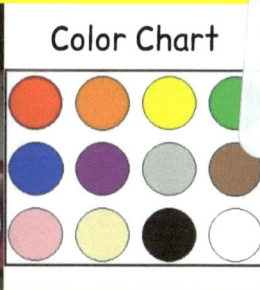

Color Chart

Ages: Infant through first grade

First Words
For New Readers

VOLUME 1
SIGHT WORDS IN CONTEXT SERIES

Your child learns frequently used (sight) words by hearing you read and by seeing the words in a very short story form on three learning levels along with color photographs.

by
Howard W. Myers
Sharon R. Myers, Managing Editor

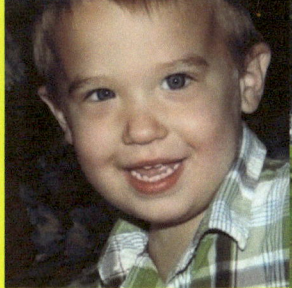

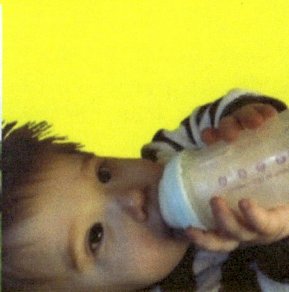

Acorn L M G, Inc.
Lil Oaks Book Group
P. O. Box 701
Crystal Lake, IL 60039

First Edition - April, 2015
First Printing - April, 2015
20 18 16 14 12 10 8 6 4 2   1 3 5 7 9 11 13 15 17 19

ISBN-13: 978-0692406618
ISBN-10: 0692406611

Acknowledgements and Credits

Your thoughtful and valuable contributions have made this book a more complete and useful work. Many, many thanks to the following people:

A. C. Myers
H. A. Myers
J. A. Myers
K. L. Myers

Subject Material

Books > Reference
Books > Children's Books > Early Learning > Basic Concepts
. . . Fun . . . Bath Time . . . Bed Time . . . Clothing
. . . Colors . . . Eating . . . Farms . . . Farm Animals
Books > Children's Books > Early Learning > Words
Books > Children's Books > Early Learning > Beginner Readers

Most of the text of this book is set in the "Comic Relief" typeface, as is this paragraph. Copyright (c) 2013, Jeff Davis (info@loudifier.com), Reserved Font Name "Comic Relief". This Font Software is licensed under the SIL Open Font License, Version 1.1. As of this printing, this font is available from www.fontsquirrel.com .

Some of the text of this book is set in the "Fjord" typeface, as is this paragraph. Copyright (c) 2011 by Sorkin Type Co. (www.sorkintype.com), with Reserved Font Name "Fjord" and "Fjord One". This Font Software is licensed under the SIL Open Font License, Version 1.1. As of this printing, this font is available from www.fontsquirrel.com .

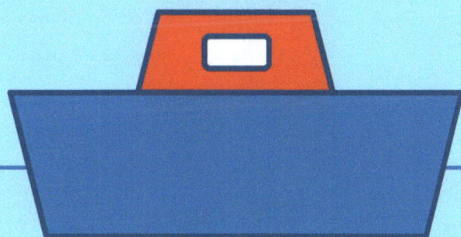

This volume has a section on each of the following:

Colors
Clothing
Eating
Fun
Bath Time
Bed Time
Farms
Farm Animals

Sharon R. Myers
Howard W. Myers

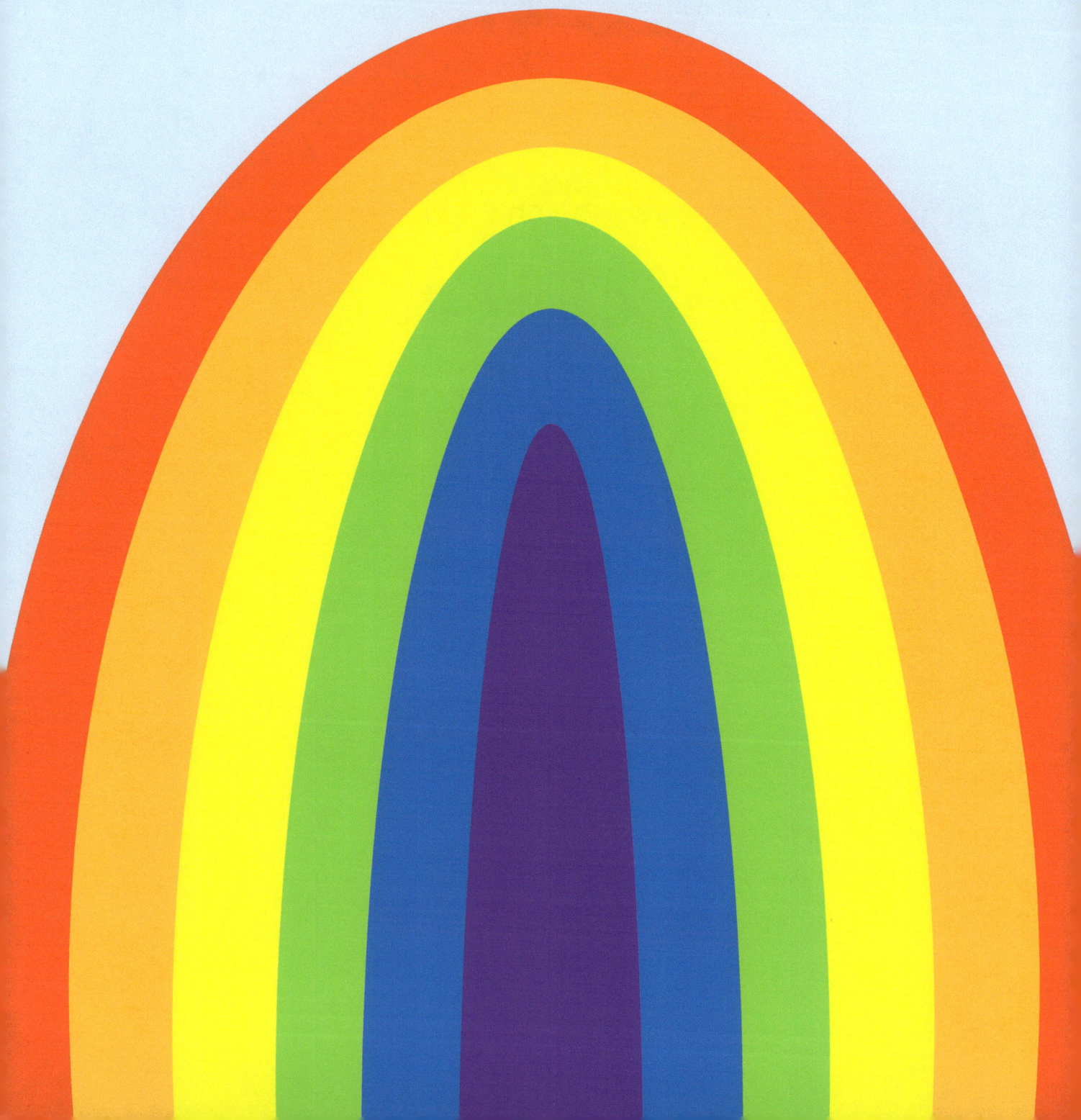

Colors

1. This is a color chart. It shows many colors.
2. It shows the most important colors.
3. In addition to these there are other colors. You will learn about them later in art class.

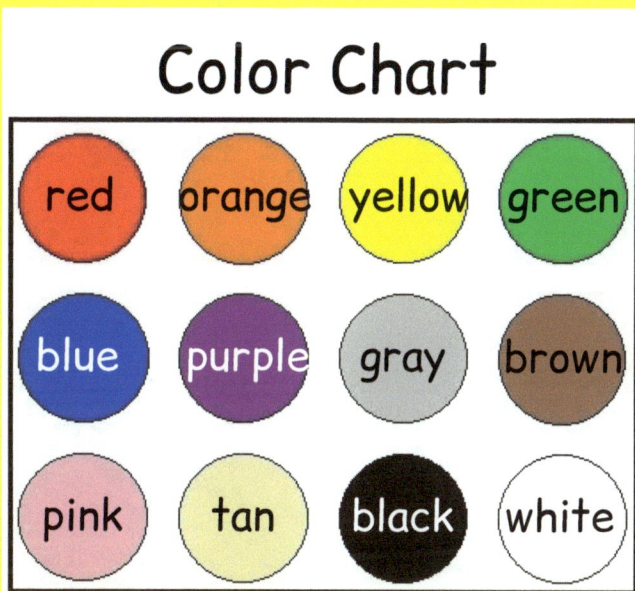

Color Chart

red	orange	yellow	green
blue	purple	gray	brown
pink	tan	black	white

1. This is my dress. It has little red and green flowers on it.
2. What colors do you see around me?
3. I see red, orange, yellow, green, blue, and purple.

1. He has a black and white shirt.
2. He is also wearing a black jacket. Besides that, he is wearing a gray hat.
3. He has the color red all around him.

1. This is a blue swimming pool.
2. See the blue sky and white clouds?
3. It is a nice place to swim when adults are present. Always wear goggles and a safety vest while swimming. Swimming lessons are also a good idea.

1. These flowers are purple.
2. They also have green leaves.
3. Each center is soft and puffy like a cotton ball.

1. This girl wants to play.
2. She is wearing a green and white dress.
3. She has a bumpy green ball.

1. This little boy is wearing a vest. The vest has stripes.
2. The vest also has a zipper.
3. He is wearing a yellow shirt under his vest. He is also holding a plastic toy yellow banana.

1. These are orange pumpkins and flowers.
2. The flowers are beautiful.
3. The pumpkins can be made into pie.

Clothing

1. My shirt is orange.
2. I am standing on a sidewalk.
   The sidewalk is made with blocks.
3. The blocks are called bricks.
   Sidewalks and buildings can be made with bricks.

1. She has a white hat.
2. She is also wearing a pink dress.
3. This fancy hat is called a bonnet.

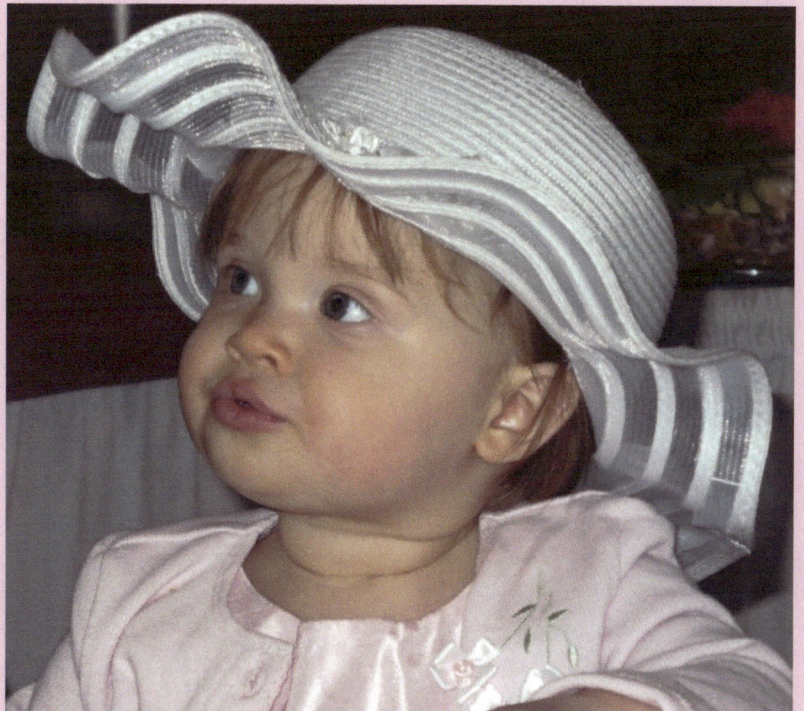

1. She is wearing a winter hat and coat.
2. They are both black with a red border.
3. These will keep her warm on a cold winter's day.

1. My shirt is red.
   I like the color red.
2. Red is a very bright color.
3. Many fire engines are also red.
   Since red is so bright, everyone notices it right away.
   When people see a bright red fire engine they can get out of the way.
   Then the fire fighters can get to the emergency more quickly.

1. She is wearing a
   green and white dress.
2. She is also wearing
   a white flower.
   She has a white bow
   in her hair.
3. And, notice her
   beautiful smile.

1. These are rain clothes.
2. Her coat is a rain coat.
3. This type of coat is
   very light weight.
   The rain coat will
   keep her dry.
   She is also wearing a
   rain hat and boots.
   She is holding an umbrella.
   The umbrella is to keep
   the rain away from her
   hair and face.

1. Her dress is pink.
2. She is having fun.
3. She is at her
   birthday party.

1 . This is a nice way to
   dress for summer.
   The lower part
   is yellow and blue.
2. This clothing will
   help her stay cool.
3. And it will help
   protect her from
   sunburn.
   A hat and
   long sleeves would
   help even more.

Eating

1. Baby drinks milk from a bottle.
2. Baby drinks milk before a nap.
3. Baby drinks milk at bed time.

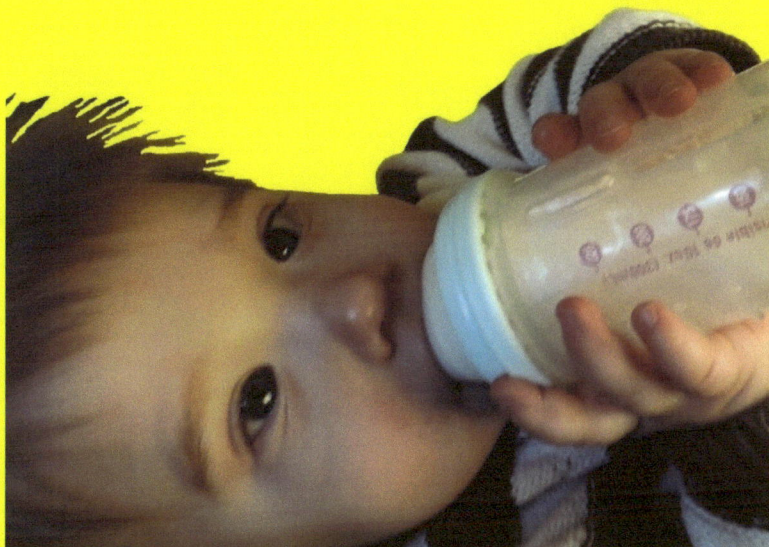

1. This is a sippy cup.
2. If this cup tips, it does not spill.
3. Sippy cups are for a child's milk or juice.

1. These are
   a fork and a spoon.
2. They are tools to
   help us eat.
3. Older children and
   adults use
   larger tools.
   These tools are
   called silverware.

1. He uses a spoon and
   bib.
2. The bib helps him
   keep his shirt clean.
3. Learning how to use
   a spoon takes time.
   It also takes
   practice.
   He is eating
   macaroni and
   cheese from a bowl.

1. This little girl is happy.
   She has milk and a cookie.
2. Most children love milk and cookies.
3. Milk and cookies are usually eaten as a snack or dessert.

1. This little boy is drinking water.
2. Water tastes good on a hot day.
3. It is important to drink enough water on a hot day in the summer.

1. These are birthday party cupcakes. There is also cold juice.
2. Ask your mom or dad before eating sweets.
3. A parent knows best about how many sweets you can eat.

1. This little girl likes pizza.
2. Pizza has a crust similar to bread. Pizza also contains tomatoes and other toppings. Some pizza contains meat and cheese.
3. Maybe that is why pizza is such a favorite food.

Fun

1. This is the best pumpkin.
2. We went to buy a pumpkin today.
   I picked this one because it is round and smooth.
   It is my favorite pumpkin.
3. This pumpkin is the one we will buy.

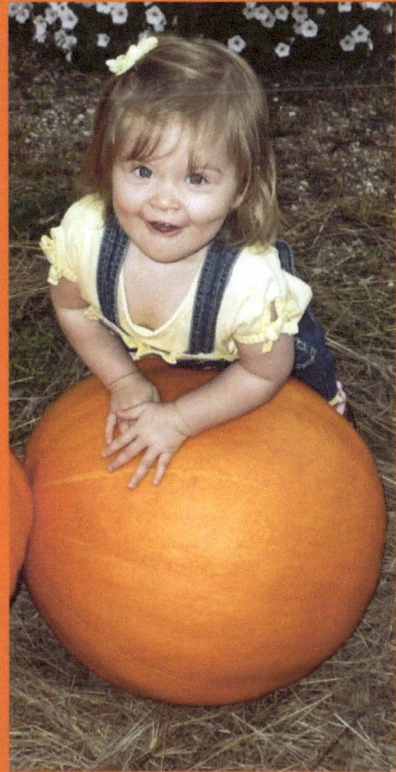

1. We are making a cookie house.
2. It is made of gingerbread.
3. It is now ready to decorate.
   White frosting and candy are added.
   White frosting looks like snow.
   Candy makes the house look festive.

1. I really like flowers.
   Can you see the
   garden behind me?
2. I am in my wagon.
   I love to be pulled
   around the garden.
3. As I am pulled
   through it, I can
   see and smell all
   the pretty flowers.

1. This ride goes
   round and round.
   It is called a
   merry-go-round.
2. It is also called a
   carousel.
3. Rides like this
   are fun.
   Adults also enjoy
   them.

1. I am ready to help Grammy bake.
2. I am measuring the sugar and other things we need. These things are called ingredients.
3. We will mix all the ingredients together. This becomes batter. Batter becomes cake when it is baked.

1. She helps Grammy make cupcakes.
2. Cupcake papers are placed into the pan.
3. Batter is spooned into the papers. This batter makes chocolate cupcakes. After baking, they are cooled. Then frosting will be put on top.

1. I am playing in my sand box.
2. I can make things from sand.
3. I can use the pail in my hand to make things from sand. Sand castles are fun to build.

1. She is riding in a boat on a river.
2. The river is usually cool in the summer.
3. She is wearing a purple safety vest. She is also having a very good time.

Bath Time

1. This is a comb.
2. A comb helps make my hair look neat.
3. I use a comb on my hair after a bath. I also use a comb when I get up in the morning.

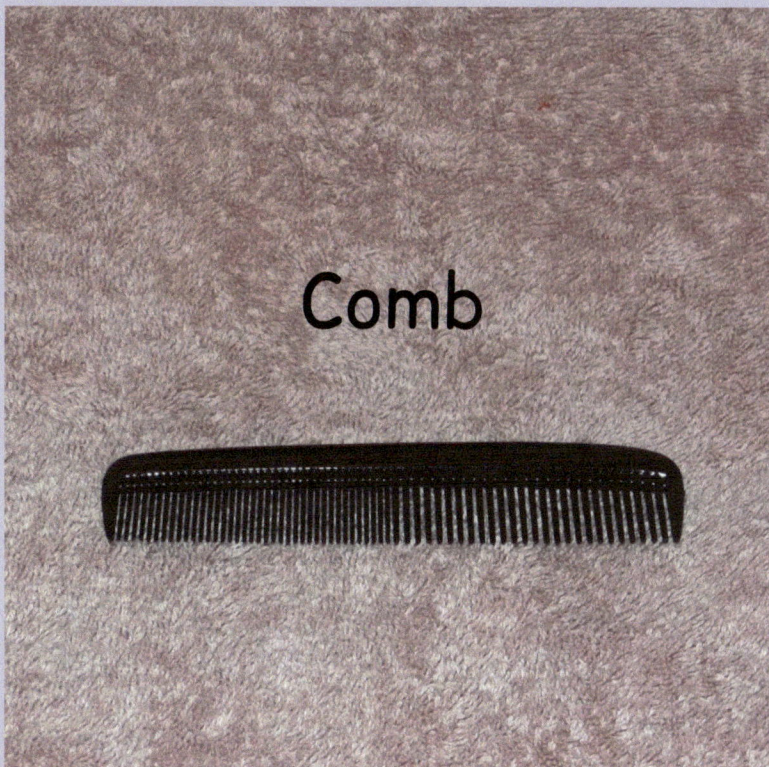

Comb

1. Here is a hair brush.
2. Some people use a hair brush to make their hair look neat.
3. They can use a brush on their hair after a bath and when they get up in the morning.

Brush

Baby
shampoo

Wash cloth

Soap

1. Here are soap,
   washcloth, and
   baby shampoo.
2. Soap and
   wash cloth are
   for body washing.
3. Shampoo is
   liquid soap for
   hair washing.
   Soon I will
   have a nice
   warm bath.

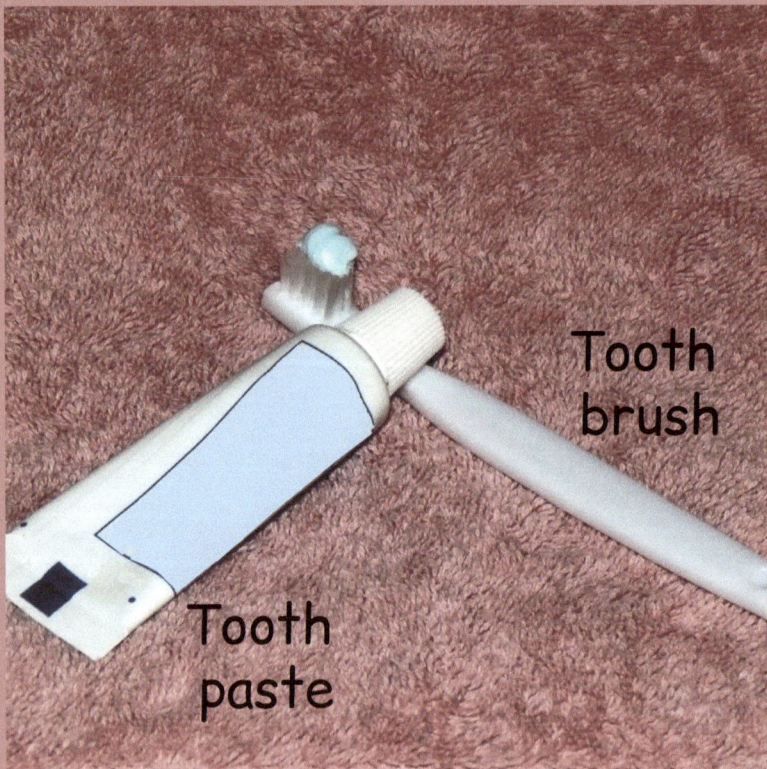

Tooth
brush

Tooth
paste

1. Here are my
   tooth brush and
   my tooth paste.
2. First, the tooth
   paste gets put on
   the tooth brush.
3. Then I brush my
   teeth up and down.
   Then I brush them
   side to side. I make
   sure that I brush
   each tooth.

1. I just had a bath.
2. I look and feel
   clean.
3. I like feeling clean.
   Being clean helps
   me to stay healthy.

1. I am drying
   my hair
   with a towel.
2. After washing
   hair, it is dried.
3. Next, I must
   comb or brush it.

1. Mommy brushed
   my hair.
2. A clip holds
   my hair in place.
3. I really like
   the way
   my hair looks.

1. This is my rubber
   duck.
2. It floats in my
   bath water.
   I have other bath
   toys, too.
3. They are a lot of
   fun at bath time.

Bed Time

1. This is my Teddy Bear.
2. Stuffed toys are very cuddly.
3. They are nice to look at before I fall asleep.

1. This is my crib.
2. I can sleep or play in this crib.
3. It folds up so it will fit in our car for travel.

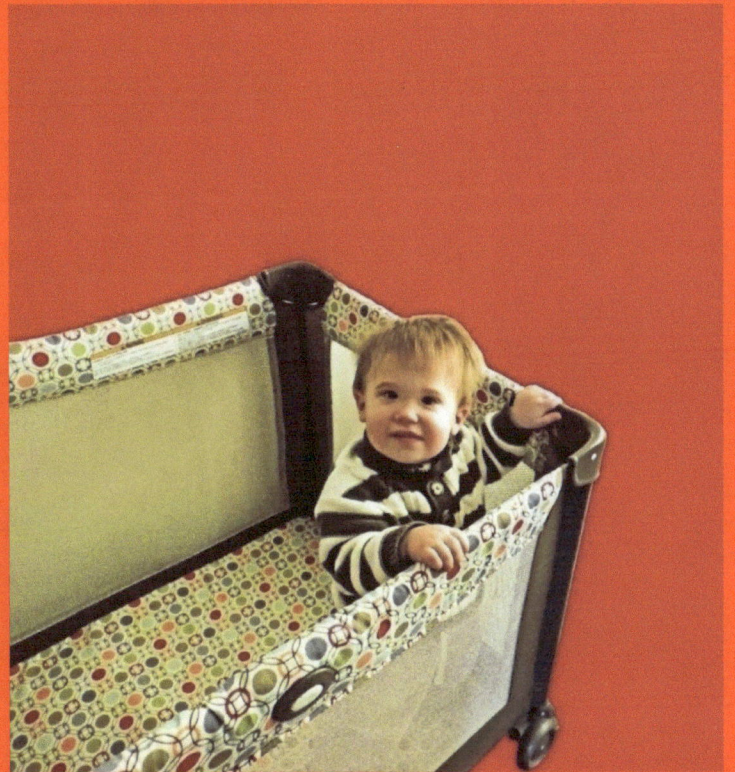

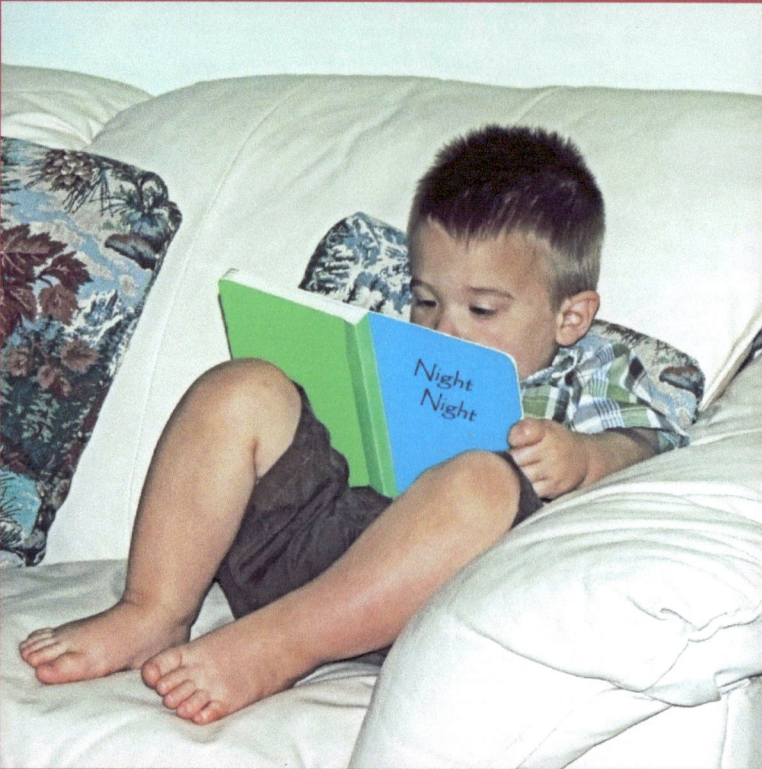

1. He is reading a book.
2. This helps him become sleepy.
3. Reading is a great way to learn.

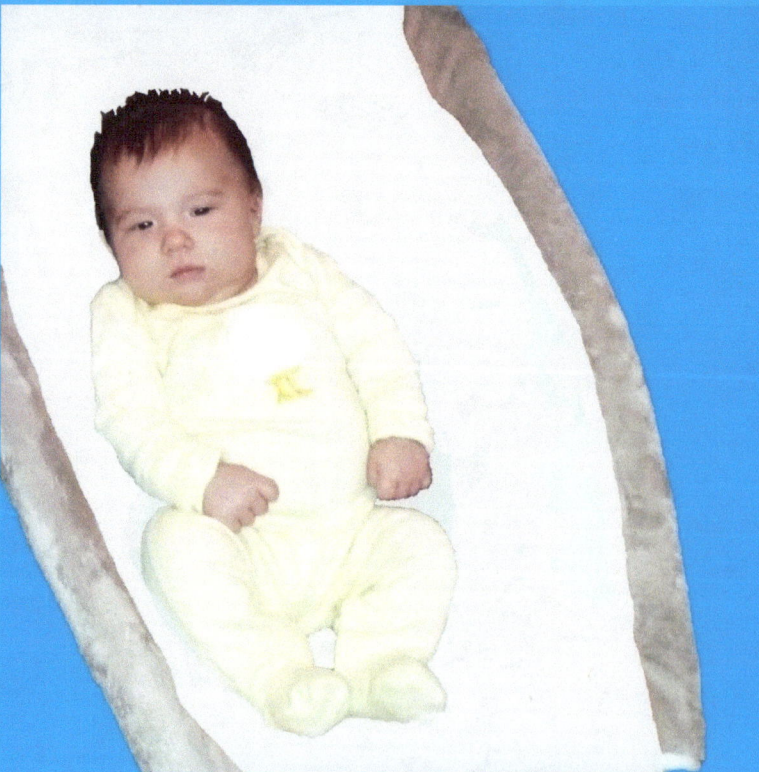

1. I am rocking in my cradle.
2. Moving back and forth makes me sleepy.
3. It is a nice way to relax and fall asleep.

1. This little boy is sleeping in his bed.
2. He has a pillow and a cover.
3. He looks very comfortable.

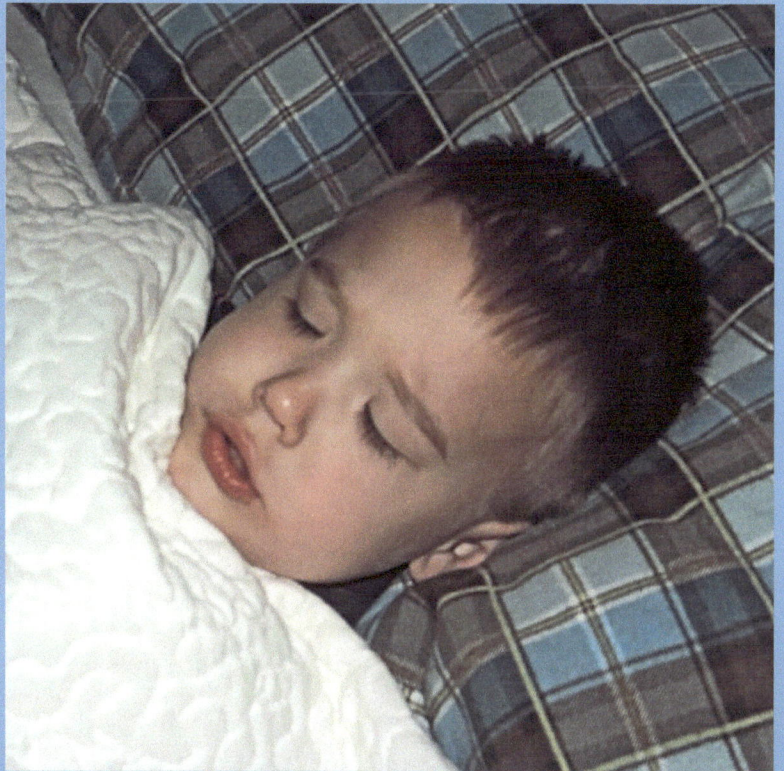

1. This is her crib.
2. She is wearing her sleeper.
3. Sleepers are very warm and comfortable.

Farms

1. This is a farm. It has a barn.
2. The barn is red.
3. Can you see the tall structure next to the barn? This is called silo. It is used to store animal feed.

1. This is a field of corn.
2. Anything planted in a farm field is called a crop.
3. Corn plants have stalks, leaves, and corn cobs with kernels. The kernels on the cobs are eaten by people. Farmers store the stalks and leaves in the silo for animal feed.

1. This is a crop of grain.
2. Some grains are: wheat, rye, and oats.
3. Wheat and rye are made into flour.
   White bread is made from wheat flour.
   So is whole wheat bread.
   Rye bread is made from rye flour.
   Oats become cereal.

1. These are rolls of hay.
2. They are very heavy.
   They must be moved using a machine.
3. Notice how each roll is wrapped in plastic.
   This keeps the hay dry if it rains.
   Hay is fed to cows, horses, and other farm animals.

1. Here is a tractor.
   It is pulling a trailer.
2. Tractors prepare the
   land for planting.
   They plant seeds, too.
   Soil is tilled while the
   crops are growing.
   Tilling helps to stop
   weeds from growing.
3. Tractors also help
   pick the crops at
   harvest time.

1. This tractor gets the
   field ready to plant.
2. Tilling turns dirt over
   to uncover fresh soil.
   The field is prepared
   for the next planting.
3. How was this work
   done before tractors
   were invented?
   Horses plowed fields.
   People picked
   the crops by hand.

Farm Animals

1. Here is a rooster. This one is pretty.
2. He has a red comb. His body is brown. His tail is black.
3. Roosters wake up early in the morning. A group of roosters is called a flock. A flock can have just a few roosters or many more.

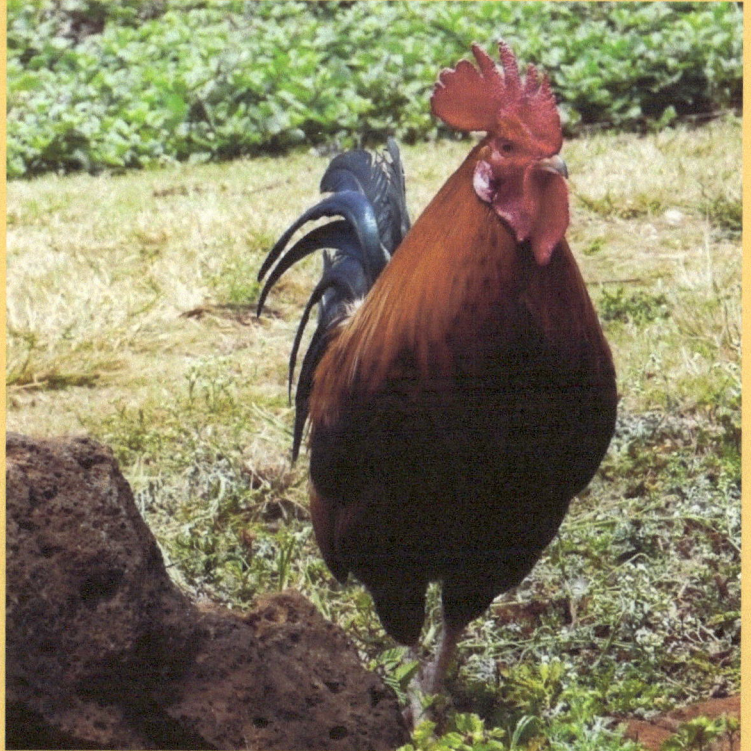

1. This is a black steer.
2. It is a strong animal. Do not go near the back legs. They can kick hard. The back legs are called the hind legs.
3. A group of steers is called a herd. A herd can have just a few or up to many hundreds of animals

1. This is a farm goose.
   This goose is white.
2. When we talk about
   one, we say goose.
   When we talk about
   more than one,
   we say geese.
3. Some geese are wild.
   Wild geese are not
   raised on farms.
   They find their own
   food, such as grass.

1. Here is a cow.
   This cow is brown.
   Cows give us milk.
   Many people drink
   cow milk and like it.
2. Cows are usually
   friendly.
   Stay away from
   their hind legs.
3. Cow herds can have
   just a few animals
   or many animals.

1. This girl has a chick.
   A chick is a baby
   chicken.
   Chicks are very fuzzy.
   This one is
   seven days old.
2. Chicks grow up to be
   hens or roosters.
3. As hens get older,
   they lay eggs.
   This begins when
   they are about a
   year old.

1. Here is a colt with
   its mother.
   A colt is
   a young horse.
2. The mother horse
   is called a mare.
3. The mare cares for
   her colt while
   it is young.
   The colt will care
   for itself when
   it grows older.

1. This is a goat.
   It is very friendly.
2. This cute little girl is
   surprised. Goats are
   usually very friendly.
3. Goats always seem
   to be hungry.
   Goats give us milk.
   Some people like
   to drink goat milk.
   Some cheese is made
   from goat milk.

1. This is a sheep.
   It is friendly.
2. When we talk about
   one, we say: sheep.
   Speaking about many,
   we also say: sheep.
   So, we could say:
   this is a nice sheep.
   If we had 5 of them,
   we could say: these
   five sheep are nice.
3. Sheep give us wool.
   Wool coats are warm.

Sight Words: Background

What are "sight words" and how they originate? Well, sight words are words we use every day. In fact, they are the words most frequently used in English language printed materials. Since we come across them so often, it behooves us and our new readers to learn and recognize them on sight.

This is especially necessary for our young readers, who are just learning how to "decode" or attach sound and meaning to those unfamiliar (to them), strange looking sets of symbols (letters), which we call words. If they do not learn to immediately recognize these words, and try to decode one every time they see one, it will likely slow down their reading speed and comprehension.

Various studies have been carried out to determine which words occur most frequently in English writings. One of these studies involved 500 word samples from each of 1,000 books, plus samplings from magazines, newspapers, and other print media. That was a word sample of half a million words. Then, the research team derived what statisticians call a frequency distribution. This was done by first finding each unique word in the entire sample collection. Then, the entire collection was examined to count the number of occurrences of each word. (This is known as the frequency of the word.) When these word-frequency pairs are sorted, the word with the largest frequency is the most common word in the entire collection. "The" is the most frequently used word in the English language.

Some very interesting results came out of these studies. Of course, since each researcher used his/her own selection of printed materials, the results were not identical for each research project. However, the results were materially very similar.

This research revealed that the top ten highest usage words (the, and, to, is, that, of, a, in, it, you) comprise about 25% of the total number of words in all printed material. The top 25 words make up about 33% of what we read and the top 100 words constitute about 50% of all reading material. So, just imagine how much more reading literacy we can achieve just by knowing and instantly recognizing those top 100 words. There are other reasons which favor instant recognition of high frequency words. A significant number of them are especially difficult to decode because of their spellings, for example.

Educators feel strongly that it is better to learn sight words in the context of sentences or a story, rather than by themselves on flash cards and the like. That has been one of the main motivating factors for writing this book in this format - sentences, very short stories, and pictures.

Many Thanks . . .

We sincerely thank you for purchasing our book. We hope that you and your child are finding it to be beneficial. We want it to be educational for your child. We also hope that it gives you and your child a pleasant way to spend time together.

We would appreciate any and all feedback from you. This can be done through email (acornhoward@yahoo.com). Or, if you are inclined to write a brief (or thorough) review, you are invited to post one on the Amazon.com website.

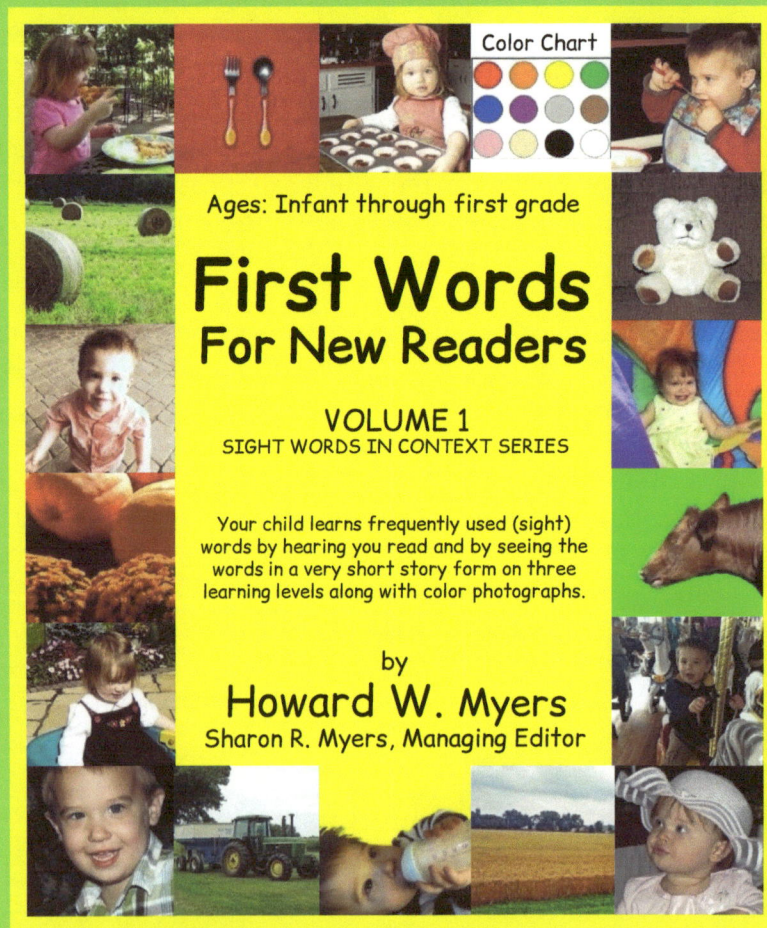

Color Chart

Ages: Infant through first grade

First Words
For New Readers

VOLUME 1
SIGHT WORDS IN CONTEXT SERIES

Your child learns frequently used (sight) words by hearing you read and by seeing the words in a very short story form on three learning levels along with color photographs.

by

Howard W. Myers

Sharon R. Myers, Managing Editor

Biographical Information

During and after a 25 year long computer science-oriented career, Howard taught at the middle school, high school, college, and graduate school university levels. Sharon founded and managed a successful newsletter business for over twenty years while serving as general manager of Howard's consulting firm. This book project combines Howard's passions for teaching and learning with his love of photography and employs Sharon's knack for proofreading, editing, and formatting.

Sharon and Howard have been married for 49 years and raised two fine sons. They now are blessed with two wonderful grandchildren. Besides children and grandchildren, Sharon's interests are in antiques, reading, and the culinary arts. Howard likes birdwatching, raising chickens, and has been an avid photographer for more than 50 years. Howard and Sharon live in the midwest.

Howard

Sharon

Ordering Information . . .

First Words For New Readers may be obtained from the Amazon.com and the CreateSpace.com web sites. This book is also available by contacting the publisher, whose information appears below.

Large quantity orders for this book can be placed through normal distribution channels or directly with the publisher, by schools, libraries, and other educational institutions.

The contact information for the publisher follows:

Acorn LMG, Inc.
Lil Oaks Publishing Group
P. O. Box 701
Crystal Lake, IL 60039
or via email at AcornHoward@yahoo.com

- Thank you -

EASY ORDER FORM

email orders: AcornHoward@yahoo.com

Postal orders: Acorn LMG, Inc.
                Lil Oaks Publishing Group
                P. O. Box 701
                Crystal Lake, IL 60039

Please send the following books and other publications:
I understand that I may return any of them for any reason.

   Quantity   Title or ISBN

_____

_____

_____

Please send more FREE information about:
__Other Books   __Seminars/Speaking   __Consulting

Your Name: _____

Address: _____

City: _____ State: _____ ZIP: _____

Telephone: _____

Email address: _____

Sales tax: Please add 7.5% for books shipped to Illinois.
Shipping (2 day): $4. for first book, plus $2. per additional.

This page has been left blank.

www.ingramcontent.com/pod-product-compliance
Lightning Source LLC
Chambersburg PA
CBHW041236040426
42445CB00004B/45